Getting the Hang of Fashion and Dress Codes

Other titles in the series Life—A How-to Guide

Choosing a Community Service Career
A How-to Guide
Library ed. 978-1-59845-147-4
Paperback 978-1-59845-312-6

Dealing With Stress
A How-to Guide
Library ed. 978-0-7660-3439-6
Paperback 978-1-59845-309-6

Friendship
A How-to Guide
Library ed. 978-0-7660-3442-6
Paperback 978-1-59845-315-7

Getting Ready to Drive
A How-to Guide
Library ed. 978-0-7660-3443-3
Paperback 978-1-59845-314-0

Using Technology
A How-to Guide
Library ed. 978-0-7660-3441-9
Paperback 978-1-59845-311-9

Volunteering
A How-to Guide
Library ed. 978-0-7660-3440-2
Paperback 978-1-59845-310-2

Getting the Hang of Fashion and Dress Codes

Life
A
How-to
Guide

A
How-to
Guide

Tom Streissguth

Enslow Publishers, Inc.

40 Industrial Road
Box 398
Berkeley Heights, NJ 07922
USA

http://www.enslow.com

Library of Congress Cataloging-in-Publication Data

Streissguth, Thomas, 1958-
  Getting the hang of fashion and dress codes : a how-to guide / Tom Streissguth.
    p. cm.—(Life—a how-to guide)
  Includes bibliographical references and index.
  Summary: "Read about the history of fashion, current fashion trends, and dress codes"—Provided by publisher.
  ISBN 978-0-7660-3444-0
  1. Fashion—United States—History—Juvenile literature. 2. Clothing and dress—United States—History—Juvenile literature. I. Title.
  GT605.S77 2011
  391.00973—dc22

                    2010033037

Paperback ISBN 978-1-59845-313-3

Printed in the United States of America

072011 Lake Book Manufacturing, Inc., Melrose Park, IL

10 9 8 7 6 5 4 3 2 1

To Our Readers: We have done our best to make sure all Internet addresses in this book were active and appropriate when we went to press. However, the author and the publisher have no control over and assume no liability for the material available on those Internet sites or on other Web sites they may link to. Any comments or suggestions can be sent by e-mail to comments@enslow.com or to the address on the back cover.

♻ Enslow Publishers, Inc., is committed to printing our books on recycled paper. The paper in every book contains 10% to 30% post-consumer waste (PCW). The cover board on the outside of each book contains 100% PCW. Our goal is to do our part to help young people and the environment too!

Illustration Credits: Clipart from Shutterstock.com and © 2011 Clipart.com, a division of Getty Images. All rights reserved.; Advertising Archive/Courtesy Everett Collection, p. 29; AP Images/Jaime Puebla, p. 97; AP Images/John T. Burns, p. 22; Barbara Nitke/© Bravo/Courtesy Everett Collection, p. 89; Everett Collection, pp. 74, 17; Eyewire, p. 116; H. Armstrong Roberts/Classicstock/Everett Collection, p. 70; © Hedda Gjerpen/iStockphoto.com, p. 12; Mary Evans Picture Library/Everett Collection, p. 14; Mary Evans/Ronald Grant/Everett Collection, p. 37; Mirrorpix/Courtesy Everett Collection, p. 68; © North Wind Picture Archives/Alamy, p. 6; Nils Jorgensen/Rex Features/Courtesy Everett Collection, p. 26 (bottom); Paul Prescott/Shutterstock.com, p. 94; Photo by Ilpo Musto/Rex Features/Courtesy Everett Collection, p. 26 (top); © 2011 Photos.com, a division of Getty Images. All rights reserved., pp. 52, 107; Shutterstock.com, pp. 1, 3, 10, 24, 33, 41, 48, 54, 57, 59, 62, 64, 79, 86, 110.

Cover Illustration: Shutterstock.com (teen holding pink shirt).

Contents

An artist's conception of what prehistoric people may have looked like; early clothes probably consisted of animal hides.

Why Fashion?

People usually have to wear clothing most of the time. If you're not naked, you're into fashion.
Unless you have to wear some kind of uniform to school or to work, you're probably wearing a style that you chose, first at the store and then from your closet. The choice all depends on you. Do you want to dress preppy, punk, goth, emo, skater, retro, or in a style all your own? Whatever you put on, that's your look. It's how you want the world to see you.

Fashion is big business. People spend a lot of money on clothes, shoes, and accessories. The market for clothing includes *everybody*—young or old, rich or poor, tall or short, fat or thin. The industry depends on the fact that people want to look good. It also depends on trends changing from year to year and season to season. If clothing didn't go out of style, clothing companies wouldn't make as much money. People would just keep wearing the same clothes year after year. The fashion business needs styles to become trendy and fall out of favor when new trends develop. Old styles then get put on discount in bargain basement stores, or they get pushed to the back of your closet.

The First Fashion Trend

It all began with some caveman or cavewoman on a dark night, a very long time ago. Sitting next to a dying fire and really feeling the chill, the caveman decided to throw something on to keep warm. It might have been a shaggy little fur pelt, or the rough hide of a mammoth lying in the corner of the cave. Eventually the cave dwellers figured out how to cut and sew together pieces of clothing. By digging in prehistoric campsites, archaeologists have discovered that about forty thousand years ago, with the development of the Cro-Magnon men, or modern humans, the first sewing kits were made with sharp implements of bone and antler.

Everyone wanted to keep warm, of course, and a nice thick pelt was just the thing. Another early human, admiring her friend's pelt, may have felt that first twinge of fashion envy. The trend eventually moved to leather hides—the skins of animals, with the fur sheared off. This was not the best part of the animal for eating, but it could be cut and shaped. The hides could be wrapped around the body, or tied around the feet to protect the heels and soles. A sleeveless leather tunic never went out of style. A trend began, but the first clothes weren't very comfortable. (Fashion Rule One: Good clothes have to be comfortable. The rule about "not looking fat" came later.)

Foot comfort was important, too. Shoes developed from the leather coverings used for the feet. Keeping the bottom of the foot covered protected it from sharp stones and let one run faster when hunting or when running away from someone else. The leather was tied on with animal sinew. Prehistoric-era shoemakers might have tried variations for the sake of excitement and for earning a little extra in trade or shiny stones. One new style closed the bottom of the shoe around the foot, while the top of the shoe stayed open. This style lives on as cool leather sandals at the beach and flip-flops tossed into the back of a million closets.

The Working Man's Skirt

It was hot in ancient Egypt, where nearly everyone worked outdoors. People didn't really need clothes at all, and many farmers, herders, slaves, and miners worked in their birthday suits. Others felt at least a little modesty and put on a loincloth. This was a bit of cloth or leather tied around the waist with a flap hanging down in front. For a little more modesty, the flap could be extended and drawn up around the back.

Loincloths changed over time. By the Middle Kingdom period, men were putting on loin skirts. This was a rectangular piece that went all around the waist, extended to the thighs, and was held up with a belt. It could be made of cheap material, such as reeds or grass. Nobles had tunics and robes to wear, but wearing a loin skirt was cooler—literally— and the sign of a working man in ancient Egypt.

This detail from a fresco shows the "short skirt" of an Egyptian worker.

Getting the Hang of Fashion and Dress Codes

Eventually cave people started to accessorize. They strung a few bones on a strip of leather and draped them around their necks. Little finger bones or sharp teeth looked good on a strap around the wrist, too. Small stones were really in demand. Polishing them would bring out a nice shine. Bling was born.

Stylin' Through the Ages

Eventually hunters and gatherers settled down and started herding and farming. Their sheep could be shorn of their wool, which could be spun and then assembled on looms to create clothing fabric. Cotton was grown in Egypt and other places, where it went into a lighter and cooler fabric. In China, country people kept silkworms on a steady diet of mulberry leaves, which were digested and excreted to produce the world's finest, softest cloth—silk.

Much later, in Italy, the Etruscans invented the toga. This was a long piece of wool draped over the shoulder. It left the right arm free so one could slash and jab with a sword, if need be. The Romans picked up on the toga after conquering the Etruscans. Eventually the toga became a peace symbol—it could only be worn when the empire was not at war (a heavier cloak was the wartime fashion). While women as well as men followed toga fashion, the laws required married women to wear a stola, a long, sleeveless toga that draped all the way to the ground. Wearing a toga with a slick pair of open-toed leather sandals became the hot fashion statement all over ancient Europe.

In many eras and places, social classes and ages were identified by their clothes. Anyone who dressed out of line could get into trouble. For instance, in Florence in 1497, the *gonfaloniere,* or head of the city, set out some guidelines for boys under the age of fourteen. They couldn't wear any gold, silver, or silk, and they couldn't wear rose or purple clothing either (except underclothes). Citizens should "live virtuously, at all times and that your sons, being virtuous in their behaviour and dress, learn virtuous and good habits which, once acquired at a tender age, will be theirs for a long time."[1]

A few centuries later, the French emperor Napoléon developed strong ideas on fashion. He wanted France to be the best in everything. He built up a huge army and marched it all over Europe, from Spain to Russia and back. At home he banned foreign clothes and textiles. Only French cloth was good enough!

Napoléon ordered all the women in his court to wear a different dress every night. They were never to wear the same dress twice. For meetings or ceremonies, Napoléon's officers had to wear fancy white silk breeches. At the palace, he ordered the fireplaces

A neoclassical sculpture of a woman in the Piazza del Popolo in Rome, Italy. Married women were required to wear the stola, a floor-length, sleeveless toga.

Getting the Hang of Fashion and Dress Codes

blocked up. On cold winter days, the enormous rooms, with their tall ceilings and marble floors, got chilly. So the women and the men put on more clothes. Through the nineteenth century, fashionable women wore long dresses and allowed their hair to grow long, although they usually went out with hair carefully arranged above the shoulders.

Napoléon lost the Battle of Waterloo in 1815, and his French empire came to an end. He may have lost Europe, but France conquered the fashion world. The French clothing industry, with the help of Napoléon's orders and rules, thrived throughout the nineteenth and twentieth centuries. Paris is still the capital of France and of the international fashion market.

The English started a few trends as well. The English dandy Beau Brummell had to be different, so he began wearing trousers. Fancy long trousers came in, and those breeches that ended just below the knee went out (you can still see them in paintings, books, and some old movies about the Revolutionary War). Mr. Brummell also came up with the men's suit (an open coat or jacket over trousers and a tie)—which later became the international symbol of having a job. In the 1840s, another trend started up in the Punjab, in the northern part of India. The Punjab was a hot place. An English officer, Lieutenant Harry Lumsden, began dying his white cotton pajamas a darker color and wearing them in the daytime. The result: khakis (which means "dust colored" in the Urdu language). A few years later, all British troops in India were wearing khaki uniforms.

An illustration from a biography of Beau Brummell shows the style he made popular: long trousers for men.

Getting the Hang of Fashion and Dress Codes

There had always been military as well as civilian fashion. A uniform marked a man as brave, valiant, and a leader. Uniforms carried their own bling: buttons, ribbons, piping (narrow stitching down the arms and legs), and fancy epaulets that rode high on the shoulders. But the military outfit was not for everyone. Henry David Thoreau, living in the woods in Massachusetts, made this early antifashion statement: "I once had a sparrow alight upon my shoulder for a moment, while I was hoeing in a village garden, and felt that I was more distinguished by that circumstance than I should have been by any epaulet I could have worn."[2]

Meanwhile, in California

Meanwhile, in California, miners were digging for gold. Fine city clothes didn't last long when working in a mine shaft, or panning for the shiny yellow flecks along a rushing mountain stream. Miners needed something a little tougher to wear. Along came a German merchant named Levi Strauss. He borrowed heavy canvas from a sailmaking shop and began making some tougher trousers.

Canvas wasn't cheap, and Strauss soon ran out. To replace it, he used *serge de Nimes,* a thick cotton cloth from Europe. Soon all the California miners were using "Levi's," made from "denim." In the 1870s, Strauss started up a new line of blue-dyed trousers that had small copper rivets sewn into them for strength. Blue jeans were work clothes, used for the outdoors.

In the Roaring Twenties (the 1920s, that is), working in the great outdoors as a rancher or carpenter or miner, in tough and durable blue jeans, wasn't very cool. Clean hands and office jobs were cool. People liked to dress as if they had a lot of free time. Jobs were easier to find for people moving into the cities, where many members of the growing middle class had enough money to live and enjoy life.

Fashion changed for women, especially in the cities. Instead of long dresses that covered the arms and everything else, the 1920s woman began wearing looser clothing and baring her arms and legs. "Flappers" danced with their arms free and flapping like a bird. Some of them drank when drinking was against the law. They wore slinky dresses and cut their hair short—a strange and shocking style to some people. Skirts rose and fell, going from the calf to the knee and then to the calf again depending on the current style. The flapper was more than a fashion statement; she was a symbol of the new freedoms enjoyed by women, who could now take all kinds of jobs, go out at night without a guy, dance like crazy, and vote.

The clothing industry began to understand how to change a trend and market clothes to millions of ordinary, not-rich people. Fashionable clothes and styles began seeping down into the middle class. Millions of people now had enough money to buy clothes and watch the trends; the market for fashion expanded from the rich to those who worked, saved, and kept a budget.

Getting the Hang of Fashion and Dress Codes

The short, loose skirt and bobbed hair of the flapper were symbols of the increased freedom of women. This photo is from the film *Synthetic Sin*, made in 1929.

Fashion Symbol

So, contrary to some opinion, fashion didn't start in the 1960s. Dress has been a marker of class and identity for millennia. Ancient societies reserved certain clothes, colors, and ornaments for certain social groups. Fashion modes have identified royalty and outcasts, soldiers and civilians, artisans and artists, aristocrats and the middle class. Dress was adapted to local environments, climate, and the seasons. It served as an emblem of age, rank, and experience.

In recent times, the lines between social classes have been shifting. This started with revolutions in France and America in the eighteenth century. By the end of the twentieth century, rigid class distinctions were pretty much gone in most countries. Social mobility means more people can dress as they wish. Although original designer clothing is expensive, most people can buy imitations or knockoffs in a discount store. The fashion market has liberated most people from social dress codes.

Clothing is still an important sign of who you are. It signifies your personal style: punk, hippie, preppy, Goth, emo, or whatever. It can also indicate your taste in entertainment—showing what kind of sports, movies, books, TV, and music that you like. Without the many rules of the past about what to wear and when to wear it, modern humans are all alone, dressing as they please, and always wondering what to put on.

Generations at the Gap

Fashion and rebellion go along together, because clothes are one way to make a statement. This rebellion has been going on for generations. Kids growing up have to show who they are and how they're different from their parents and everyone else stuck in the older generation. Sometimes that means upsetting parents, teachers, and the world in general.

Teenagers also feel a lot of peer pressure. They have to join a group and keep themselves a part of that group by following certain rules—most of them unspoken—about the way they talk, dress, and act. It has been this way for hundreds of years. Cliques form in school, and outside the school doors, gangs wander the streets. For more than a century in big cities such as New York and Los Angeles, there have been gangs, gang clothes, and gang symbols.

Gangs were common in poor neighborhoods. It was necessary for people to find protection, if they needed it, and to get that protection in the form of groups. There were many gangs, large and small, and their clothes and colors showed membership. For instance, in the 1950s, black leather jackets, blue jeans, and tattoos showed what gang a person was in. To get in and stay in, one also had to show he was willing to do some violence and break some laws. Vandalism, thievery, and assault were all acceptable ways. So was drinking and taking drugs and rumbling (fighting) in the streets with rival gangs.

Zoot Suits Cause Rumble Trouble

In El Paso, Texas, gangs overran the barrios (poor neighborhoods). The worst neighborhood in town was known as the Segundo Barrio. Poor Mexican-American families squeezed into small houses, sometimes several people to a single room. Pachucos were young men who roamed the barrio, looking for trouble, in El Paso and other cities of the West and South.

Like everyone else, pachucos wanted to dress for success. To make the right impression, they started wearing zoot suits. ("Zoot" was just another way of saying "suit.") They were made

U.S. Rules

The whole country used to have a dress code of sorts. Not too long ago, wearing trousers could get a woman in trouble. In some places, a woman could get taken down to the police station and arrested for wearing men's clothing, or wearing anything that showed her legs. In 1923, the attorney general of the United States declared that trousers were legal for women everywhere in the country. However, they were not permitted in some settings, such as school, for many decades.

up of baggy pants and narrow cuffs, suit jackets with very wide lapels and padded shoulders, pointy shoes, and floppy felt hats. It moved from El Paso to Los Angeles, where African Americans picked up on zoot suits. Needless to say, the authorities didn't approve. First, zoot suits looked like a waste of good material. Second, and more importantly, they were a sign of defiance on the part of people who should stay in their place and stop dressing up like the higher class.

The zoot suit caused trouble wherever it went. In Los Angeles, the fashion style invented by a few poor Hispanics in El Paso caused an outright riot. During World War II, rumors spread of a crime wave among Hispanics and African Americans. Sailors on leave from the war roamed the city's poor neighborhoods, attacking anyone and everyone wearing a zoot suit.

A young Hispanic man models a zoot suit inside a Los Angeles county jail in 1943. During World War II, rumors of violence among Hispanics and African Americans led to attacks on anyone wearing a zoot suit.

The *New York Times* described the action:

> The arrests came after a "war" declared by service
> men, mostly sailors, on zoot-suit gangs which have
> been preying on the East Side as well as molesting
> civilians. Impetus was given to the clean-up
> campaign when the wives of two sailors were
> criminally attacked by the youths. . . . Cruising in
> taxicabs and cars, and occasionally spearing into
> enemy territory on foot in precise platoon drill, the
> service men routed the gangs, depriving them of
> crude weapons. . . . Favored for fighting by the
> youths were lengths of rope weighted with wire
> and lead, tire chains and wrenches, hammers and
> heavy bottles, some with the tops broken off.[1]

Like other fashion trends, the zoot suit faded after a few years. New trends such as beatnik took over, and the zoot suit entered the fashion museum. There was also something new coming down the fashion road: the 60s.

The 1960s

During the 1960s, the big baby boom generation was growing up. This group was born after the end of World War II in 1945, when American soldiers came home, the economy grew, and families moved out to the suburbs. Teenagers at the time didn't have much chance at employment, but they did have "disposable" income, meaning they could spend it on clothes.

Hippies adopted a freer, more creative style of dress to reflect their beliefs about life. Long hair and tie-dyed shirts were common.

Getting the Hang of Fashion and Dress Codes

The baby boomers rebelled, naturally. People began expressing themselves in all kinds of ways. They ignored fashion advertising, marketing, and trends and just dressed in their  own way with clothes they picked up here and there. At one time, most people picked up on fashion to look rich and stylish. Now they ignored the trend in order to look different and cool. Eventually, the new look became a uniform and style of its own.

With so many young people buying clothes, the fashion industry had to respond to changes in the market. Teenagers began driving everything forward. There were new looks, costumes that everyone was trying on. Blue jeans and T-shirts came on strong. They looked less businesslike than button-down shirts.

Hippies were the symbol of the new fashion non-statement. They dropped out from the nine-to-five world and lived a different way. They appeared in  tie-dyed T-shirts, blue jeans, sandals, and long hair. They liked ethnic clothing, such as daishikis from Africa; printed skirts and shirts from India; and beads, bandannas, and moccasins adopted from the American Indians. But "being a hippie is not a matter of dress, behavior, economic status, or social milieu," as Skip Stone wrote in his 1999 book *Hippies A to Z*. "It is a philosophical approach to life that emphasizes freedom, peace, love and a respect for others and the earth. The way of the hippie never died."[2]

David Bowie (on left) was the star of glam rock, while Iggy Pop (below) was the original New York punk.

Getting the Hang of Fashion and Dress Codes

The Punk Rebellion

When the stars showed up on television with their new clothes, everyone wanted the same. The whole idea of rebelling against a norm developed into yet another norm, as fans of certain musicians showed their loyalty by dressing like the stars. David Bowie and Elton John were stars of glam rock, and the Grateful Dead were stars of another sort—the hippie look.

Then punk came along, somewhere in a quiet London neighborhood. Weird spiky hair and green mohawks terrified innocent passersby on the streets. Punks put on badly ripped T-shirts and leather clothes with chains and steel studs. The studs also showed up in dog collars that they wore around their necks (with or without a leash).

The punk look caught on in New York City. Iggy Pop was the original New York punk, along with his bandmates in the Stooges. Compared to most rock bands, they were out of control, fashionwise. "You had this skinny guy in tight jeans which were ripped and he had this great body," said one witness. "He had incredible eyes. He looked fantastic. . . . Iggy used to go out into the crowd, get in their faces, follow people around. The crowd used to reciprocate by throwing bottles at them, cameras, cans—it was generally carnage."[3]

Along with punk came grunge music and grunge fashion. The grunge look was antistyle, antifashion, antimass market. Grunge bands such as Nirvana and their fans appeared in worn-out khakis or ripped jeans, baggy flannel shirts, and absolutely no jewelry or any other adornment. Designer labels and visible logos had no place in your wardrobe if you were grungy.

Punk and grunge traveled all over the world and finally arrived in Harajuku. This neighborhood in downtown Tokyo had hundreds of little clothing stores, each with its own look. The Japanese culture was all about work and success and conforming, so Japanese kids rebelled with their clothes, and took the looks to an extreme. The punkiest punks in the world were walking around the streets of Tokyo.

Punk, glam, grunge, new wave, metal, and other trends were running hot. Some kids even rebelled by dressing preppy, with golf shirts, plaid skirts, khakis, and penny loafers. And punk didn't look too good to girls who wanted to look girly again. A single clothing company, Laura Ashley, started a trend of its own that caught on in Japan, Europe, and North America. This look had long skirts, blouses that came up to the neck, and lots of light colors and flower prints.

Getting the Hang of Fashion and Dress Codes

Laura Ashley dresses had modest
lines and pretty floral prints.

29

Dressing Prep

Preppy fashion came from a need that emerged in the 1890s. Polo players were bouncing across fields atop their galloping horses, while the loose collars of their shirts flapped in the wind. They buttoned them to the front of their shirts to keep the collars out of their faces. A designer working for Brooks Brothers, a clothing merchant, added a small permanent button to each side of the shirt neck, and made slits at the end of the collars to fasten them. The button-down shirt became an emblem of the wealthy, polo-playing class.

A few decades later, in the 1930s, René Lacoste was playing tennis in France and going by the nickname of Le Crocodile. One day, just for fun, he put a little crocodile emblem on the front of his playing shirt. It looked interesting enough, so Lacoste started up a clothing company. Millions of little crocodiles were added to the short-sleeved Lacoste shirts of preppies all over the world. Such knit shirts are now known as "polo shirts," while the original polo shirts are called "button-downs."

There were all kinds of accessories to go with the new, trendy, clean-cut style: handbags, scarves, jewelry, trinkets, and doodads. Women of all ages adopted Laura Ashley. It was definitely an anti-punk thing.

Rebellion and Retail

At the end of the twentieth century, punk went out of style and hip-hop came in. Hip-hop started in the 1980s with rap songs by the Sugarhill Gang, Run DMC, Kurtis Blow, and others. These groups used drum tracks and spoken rhyming lyrics (no singing). Break dancing was a big part of it. Hip-hop brought in new styles in clothes, shoes, and jewelry. Videos on MTV brought the hip-hop thing to the mainstream, where it remains to this day.

While hip-hop musical style spread around the world, the idea of teenage rebellion against the retail clothing industry faded out. By the late 1990s, most people were forgetting punk and grunge and buying their clothes at familiar mall stores. Younger people favored Abercrombie & Fitch, American Eagle, Aeropostale, and Gap, while J. Crew, Banana Republic, and Eddie Bauer were popular with their parents. Each place carried ready-to-wear clothes with a label, and each label had its look and its fit. Instead of adopting a favorite style, people adopted a favorite store. For people who could afford a high-fashion label, there were upscale malls with Prada, Gucci, Louis Vuitton,  and Chanel stores. Hot Topic opened up in a California mall, catering to die-hard punk and heavy metal fans. The company Web site tells the story:

In the fall of 1989, Hot Topic opened its doors in Westminster, California. We'd love to tell you it was a huge success, with hundreds of teens clawing their way into the store, but we'd be lying. Sales were disappointing. Some days we barely made a hundred bucks. . . . It was time to take a step back and re-evaluate. . . . We started buying more stuff like cross necklaces, unisex earrings and leather bracelets and got rid of hair scrunchies, men's ties and dress socks. Hot Topic found a niche and its name was music-influenced accessories. Whether it was fingerless gloves like Billy Idol or glam metal bootstraps like Poison, music was definitely the driving force behind teen fashion.[4]

Everyone knows that if you want to break away and appear different, clothing is the key. But if you're under twenty years old, you're standing in the middle of the retail clothing storm. You're setting the trends for stores, for music, and for media in general. For that reason every clothing manufacturer in the world desperately wants to find out what you like or don't like, and they're spending about as much money on research and marketing as they are on making clothes. In the fashion world, there's no clothing without marketing—the big business of learning what *you* want.

Getting the Hang of Fashion and Dress Codes

U.S. Dress

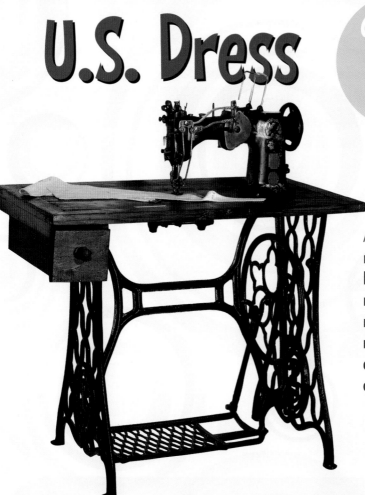

An early sewing machine, powered by foot. Sewing machines enabled many people to make their own clothes more easily.

Prior to the late 1800s, tailors had produced new clothes out of small workshops, using the fabric and designs chosen by the customer. Many people also made clothing in their homes, using their own needles and thread. Both tailor shops and many homes contained sewing machines operated by a foot treadle, which had been developed in the 1830s. Then, during the Civil War, the U.S. government had to mass-produce uniforms, so specific sizes and ready-to-wear clothing came along.

The clothing industry divided into market segments, each catering to a different customer. *Haute couture* ("high fashion") meant the original creations of the most talented designers. It was always based on an original design and made in only a few samples. People who were rich enough could buy one of these originals, but only in a few high-end shops.

Ready-to-wear and mass-market clothing were easier to find. Ready-to-wear clothing was made from original designs in large lots, in specific sizes, and sold through retail stores. Mass-market clothing was less expensive than ready-to-wear. The manufacturers copied original designs in less expensive fabrics. This clothing came in standard sizes and carried labels, each meaning something to the smart buyer. Famous designers lent their name and ideas to the company that produced the clothing. Clothing was made for two seasons, and the style changed from spring to fall and back to spring again. Beginning in the late twentieth century, designers came out with shoes, luggage, jewelry, perfumes, hats, scarves, bedspreads, and handbags. Shoppers could browse catalogs of hundreds of products, all

Getting the Hang of Fashion and Dress Codes

with the same logo and label. They could buy Ralph Lauren cologne or Eddie Bauer cars. Much of the brand-name clothing carried the logo in letters large and small, so customers became walking billboards to advertise the goods to other customers. Aeropostale, Hilfiger, and Hollister shirts strolled down the street and around the mall. This branding helped companies to sell more products to the customers who developed loyalty to a single company, a brand identified by a logo and a look.

Brand-name clothing and accessories spread around the world. Clothing companies became independent retail nations, with repeat customers becoming their citizens and company logos their flags. The market crossed all ages and cultures, from adults to teenagers and children. Even infants have brand-name clothing, and kids begin to develop personal style by the time they start school.

Madonna Sets a Trend

Back in the 1980s, the fashion was following the music. MTV was getting started. It was a new idea—just play music videos on a cable television channel, twenty-four hours a day. MTV gave new rock bands and their clothes more exposure. Instead of just playing in clubs and hoping they would be discovered, the bands could send a video to MTV and hope it got on the air. The better produced the video was, the better the chances it would make it on TV. And production was all about appearance: clothes, hair, set design, editing, and all the rest. It was a certain "look" you could identify—grunge, punk, glam rock, metal, or whatever. In a music video, visuals were the first thing to take a viewer's interest. The next was a simple story line. Then, music.

Madonna was the queen of pop music and MTV. Her first song, "Everybody," came out on a record with no picture of her and no description. She sounded like a black singer, the studio decided, so they kept her image out of the public and pitched the song to black radio stations. For a very short time, nobody knew who she was or what she looked like.

In fact, she was the daughter of a middle-class Italian-American family from the suburbs of Detroit, Michigan. She rebelled with clothes, hair, and shoes because she didn't feel very cool:

> I cut my hair really short and I'd grease it so it
> would be sticking up, and I'd rip my tights so there
> were runs all over them, and I'd make a big cut
> down the middle of my leotard and put teeny little
> safety-pins all the way up it. Anything to stand out
> and say, "I'm not like you, OK?"[1]

After leaving home, Madonna spent some very hungry times in New York City, trying to make a living as a dancer and backup singer. She was broke and wearing whatever cheap ragged clothes she could find at thrift shops. Leggings, ripped jeans, lacy blouses, corsets, different-colored shoes, fingerless gloves, crucifixes, khakis—and sometimes a little of everything thrown together at once.

Getting the Hang of Fashion and Dress Codes

Madonna in 1991. The symbol of rebellion of many teen girls, she reinvented her style many times during her career.

Madonna's first solo album came out in 1983 and hit number one on the charts—as did the next three. She appeared in clubs and in music videos and in a short time was the best-selling female rock star in history. She had a look that millions of girls picked up on: lace and leather; beads, belts, and crosses; bustiers and girlish ribbons; short skirts, boots, fishnet stockings; and bedraggled, bleached hair. Madonna's look and wardrobe changed from one tour to the next. The parents of girls did not approve of Madonna, but parents can't stop fashion.

To a lot of teenagers, Madonna meant more than cool clothes. She was a symbol of girls-only rebellion in the music scene and in the rest of the world, where men always seemed to be setting down the rules and taking the front of the stage. She did not apologize for any of the controversy she stirred up. Girls admired her fearlessness. A girl named Carmen R. explains why:

> When I was growing up in Puerto Rico . . .
> Madonna was an icon of teenage female rebellion.
> . . . Madonna gave my generation a slap in the face
> and made most of us stop and rethink the
> traditional roles we were expected to perform in
> society, pushing us beyond the conventional
> rebellion that many teenage girls go through.[2]

The clothes were cool, but the hair was the secret weapon. Men and women wore their hair straight and long in the 1960s (except those with curly hair who "went natural"). In the 1970s, hair could be worn straight and long or fluffy and feathered.

Getting the Hang of Fashion and Dress Codes

In the 1980s New Wave haircut style, girls cut it short in front and longer on the back and sides, sometimes longer on one side than the other. Mousse and gel enabled guys with short hair to make it straight and a little spiky. The goal was to not look like a hippie from the 1960s. If a person still wanted to be a little hippie, he wore a mullet, with hair cut very short on the top and sides and left to grow shaggy and long in the back.

As in all other times, a fashionable uniform came into style. The key was a pair of tight-fitting, acid-washed jeans, sold for a higher price at a fancier store than ordinary jeans. These pants went through a chemical bath that took away the blue dye in the top layer of fabric, revealing patches of the bleached white thread underneath. Every single pair of acid-washed jeans looked a little different—it was a rebellion against the sameness of ordinary blue jeans. Acid-washing could be used on jean jackets too, and in other colors beside blue.

In the meantime, new female pop stars are setting the trends for modern teens. They no longer look to Madonna for fashion inspiration, but the Madonna attitude survives. Every female music and style celebrity has a little bit of Madonna in her, from Britney Spears to Pink to Lady Gaga.

A Rap on Hip-Hop

In the 1970s, street gangs in New York were partying with boom boxes and break dancing, a way to fight without fighting. When they didn't feel like dancing, they would play word games such as the Dozens. The object of the Dozens is to humiliate your opponent with clever taunts, insulting comebacks, and nasty references to mothers and family members. The Dozens is combat by speaking. It's big on urban street corners, where people respect anyone who can speak out, rhyme, and rap.

A small-time record producer named Sylvia Robinson thought about setting this repartee to a simple drum track and a familiar bass line. She lined up three amateur musicians from Englewood, New Jersey, had them write some lyrics, and borrowed the riff from "Good Times," a song by the band Chic. The group called itself the Sugarhill Gang from the name of her record label, Sugarhill Records. In 1980, "Rapper's Delight" came out, ran way up the charts, and sold a few million copies. This was how rap music got started.

Rap music was a whole new approach to performance. Speaking lyrics instead of singing them got attention. It was weird and startling, and so was music without live guitars, horns, drums, or any other instruments (not to mention intros, verses, choruses, breaks, improvisations, chord changes, or melodies). It was pretty easy to do—all one needed was a microphone and a bass or a drum track sampled on a tape cassette. Some rappers wrote their lyrics down, while others

Hip-hop style went through many evolutions, from disco shirts to bling to saggy pants to athletic gear. Sideways baseball caps and do-rags were also popular.

just made up the words as they went along. They ran the rhythm tracks through a boom box or a PA system. It was African-American karaoke with street slangy insults, boasts, and rhymes, and with people dancing instead of sitting.

After rap music went into professional studios, and rappers started writing original rhythms and lyrics, the music caught on fast. Rap performers showed up in clubs and signed contracts with record labels, selling a lot of music to a growing audience. By the time the New Wave group Blondie did a rap song on one of their albums, rap was going mainstream.

Hip-Hop: The Clothes

Hip-hop was the whole new style that came out of rap. Rappers wore loose disco shirts, bomber jackets, athletic jerseys, big sunglasses, and baseball caps turned backward or to the side. Adidas, Nike, and Doc Martens appeared on rapper feet, and hairstyles included the Jheri curl (like Ice Cube) or a high-top (think young Will Smith). Hip-hop stars got into the heavy gold chains and earrings, nameplates hung around their necks, and big belts.

Then loose baggy pants came in. MC Hammer wore harem pants that made him look like he was wearing a tent. Then came gangsta rap, where the whole idea was to imitate the look in prison, where they don't let you wear a belt. Along with the sagging pants came tattoos, gang signs, and bandannas in certain colors wrapped around the head. The controversial hip-hop style has endured and become popular in thousands of high schools all over America. But because the clothes are like those that gang members wear, they have been banned in many schools.

Symbols of professional sports teams were big in hip-hop. NWA and other groups got into Starter jackets, favoring black-and-white team logos from the Oakland Raiders or Chicago White Sox. Michael Jordan wore Nike shoes, and everyone who wanted to be a star jock or even a playground hoops player wore them, too. For many years Jordan was the biggest star with the biggest shoe contract. For professional athletes, big bucks came from shoe and other endorsements as well as achievements on the field or the court.

Spotting a trend, fancy fashion companies took up hip-hop in the 1980s and 1990s. Not long after they wore something new on the stage or in a video, hip-hop artists spotted their gear in the mall or at Target. Chanel and Gucci brought out some fancy, high-end hip-hop clothes. Fashion houses loved the brand-name chic: Hilfiger, DKNY, and others didn't mind having their logos on shirts, sweaters, jackets, and accessories, especially up on the stage or on MTV. Gangsta clothes, or an imitation of them, showed up on the runway at exclusive shows, where magazine editors and fashion designers met to set the new trend. From the Bronx, hip-hop spread all over the world and started to hit the mainstream.

Athletes and Fashion

The world's biggest fashion success didn't come out of a fancy designer's shop in Paris. It came from a more humble place: the basketball court. In 1917, men playing basketball found street shoes unfit for sliding, weaving, and sidestepping around the court. So Marquis Converse, owner of the Converse Rubber Shoe Company, invented the Converse All-Star basketball shoe. It was made of canvas tops and rubber on the bottom. When basketball star Chuck Taylor started wearing them, the shoes really took off. Chuck Taylors were the basketball shoe of choice for a couple of generations.

Then a little Oregon shoe company called Nike ("victory" in Greek) started making Blazers and putting their Swoosh logo on them. Nike, Puma, and Converse battled it out through the 1970s. Magic Johnson and Larry Bird wore Converse Weapons, but then Nike came out with Air Force 1, the first shoe with an air sole. When Michael Jordan began playing in Air Jordans, it was game over for a while. But Adidas and Reebok were still competing. Each company hired star players to represent them. Michael Jordan played for Nike; Kobe Bryant wore Adidas for a while, then switched to Nike. Nike also sponsored Yao Ming when he was a teenager playing in China, but Ming switched to Reebok after coming to the United States. Many athletes earn about as much in shoe endorsements as they do playing basketball. The association of athletes with labels and fashion marketing continues with golfers, baseball players, and even snowboarders wearing logos, doing commercial spots, and making money.

School boards, though, didn't like hip-hop style. They wanted to avoid any fashion trend that meant distraction and disruption, and anything that tempted robbery, such as expensive brand-name shoes and jackets. The association with criminal gangs and gang violence wasn't good either. Many school districts banned gang insignia, the use of bandannas and do-rags on the head, heavy jewelry (especially gold chains), and designer sunglasses. Some prohibited hats altogether. Baggy pants were out, too. There wasn't much schools could do about hoodies, however. In a cold climate, too many people wore hoodies just to keep warm.

Emo Comes and Goes

In the 2000s, hip-hop trends changed again. Instead of oversize athletic jerseys and super-baggy shorts, tight blue jeans and T-shirts took over. Some hip-hop dressers went all the way back to button-down shirts and preppy-style polos worn with chains and wide belts, big sunglasses, and baseball caps. Two of the biggest performers, Kanye West and Usher, always looked elegant in dark shades and dark sportcoats (no ties). Diddy, Jay-Z, Eminem, and 50 Cent started their own fashion lines, appearing at mall stores all over the world.

When nostalgia kicks in, current fashion gets old. Hip-hop was going out as neo-preppy was coming in, along with the dark-colored and ironic emo look. An anonymous philosopher writing for an emo Web site described the emo attitude:

Emo is an abbreviation for emotional hardcore and claims a critical and punk attitude, but [is] centered mainly on individual, personal and private emotions, rather than on the political. Emo takes on the urban, iconoclastic street attitude of Punk, with its anger and way of expressing discontent with a reality that urges change as soon as possible. However, incorporated also in the discourse are personal feelings and emotions that, without losing clarity, and being radical and urgent, not only speak of an external malaise, but also of the pain, anger and dissatisfaction of those who do not now believe in the American Dream. This attitude . . . is shared by the whole Grunge movement, [which] defines the American way of life as nothing but a farce which pushes youth to desperation, unemployment, apathy, ignorance and loss of hope for the future. Emo raises itself against all this.[3]

The world perceived emos as being pretty deep. They were kind of punky, hardcore, and down-to-earth all at the same time. They were almost like a hippie–punk hybrid. They liked certain musical groups, of course, including Fugazi, Rites of Spring, Dag Nasty, and Weezer. But all kinds of musical styles went into emo, including industrial, post-pop, indie rock, and punk. The new wave of emo dressers made it a point to show no brand loyalty to bands or clothing.

Getting the Hang of Fashion and Dress Codes

One Web site offers some emo dressing pointers:

The Emo Romulan look—short, thick, greasy, dyed-black hair with bangs cut straight across the forehead, and cut high over the ears . . . horn-rim glasses, or at least thick black frames . . . bald head, furry face (boys only) . . . heavy slacks, often too tight and short . . . thin, too-small polyester button-ups in dark colors, or threadbare children's size t-shirts with random slogans . . . clunky black shoes . . . scarves . . . too-small cardigans and v-neck sweaters . . . argyle . . . anorexic thinness.[4]

At first, emo was an anti-statement. It was a look in which one could pretty much throw on what she wanted, as long as it wasn't fashionable (and definitely not hip-hop). But then the antistyle turned into a style. Certain colors and cuts seemed, for some reason, to work better than others. Vans and Converse sneakers worked, Nikes didn't. Flannel shirts were out. White socks were OK, and so were rolled-up tight trousers, but bell-bottom jeans or shorts—nope. Kitschy T-shirts, service-station shirts with the name sewn in, wallet chains, and pea coats all got to be standard emo gear. Badly cut and

Emo style includes tight pants and dark-rimmed glasses, as well as scarves and too-small sweaters.

Getting the Hang of Fashion and Dress Codes

combed hair looked good with it, too. That's the way fashion goes: every look develops its own rules, even though nobody seems to be writing the rules.

Emo is still cool, but it's on the way out. What's next? One fashion theory says that in hard times, people like to look wealthy in order to stand out and get noticed. In the 1930s, there was a Great Depression, and many people were out of work and out of money. For entertainment, there were cheap movies, many of which were musicals. The champagne flowed and the stars dressed in expensive suits and ball gowns. On the other hand, in good times, teenagers dress down, as a protest.

If the years to come bring hard times again, with few jobs or little money around, the polo-playing neo-preppy look may rule. Cardigan sweaters and leather loafers could come back, and all traces of punk, grunge, and emo could turn into leftovers and move to the back of the closet. Girls may put on dresses and long-sleeved blouses, and guys may wear button-down shirts and ironic neckties. The look will be just a reminder of preppy, combined with some other clothing wave, such as skater style. A music star will come along and dress that way every time he or she appears on TV. Parents and teachers will not approve, and the next fashion wave will break across the world.

Chapter 4

What's Your Style?

Dressing is expressing. The right clothes make you feel confident and cool. Everyone has his or her own style, and dressing that way makes life a little easier.

When you start picking out clothes in the morning, you start to get a style together. When you start spending your own money for clothes, that's when things really get interesting.

Preppy

This look is button-down shirts, polo shirts with long or short sleeves, Lacoste shirts (or imitators), turtleneck sweaters or V-neck sweaters over T-shirts, khakis, pleated skirts, plaid designs, and moccasins or loafers (with a penny or some other coin stuck in). Ball caps and sandals are out, and so is a lot of jewelry, but strings of pearls are standard, subdued preppy bling. Hilary Duff dresses preppy a lot. It's a nice, neat look that's easy to do because preppy clothes have a standard look, colors, and cut. People who dress preppy don't have to be creative in putting their clothes on every morning.

For men and women dressing in the preppy manner, there are rules. Women should match their handbags with their shoes and favor skirts over pants. Men should match their shoes with their belts and of course never wear any kind of hat inside. Preppies wear a bit of gold or silver jewelry, but never both. Prep style follows the season—white shoes appear only in the summer and go back into the closet on Labor Day.

"Prep" stands for preparatory school. This outfit came from exclusive private schools with strict dress codes. Students could buy their uniforms only at certain stores. Every male wore the same tie, and females wore the same skirt. Most prep students came from wealthy families, and they were "preparing" for a career at an Ivy League school. Parents took care of their needs. There was a strict preppy code, and preppies were supposed to be smart in class and good at tennis and other expensive

Polo shirts exemplify preppy style.

Getting the Hang of Fashion and Dress Codes

suburban sports—lacrosse, skiing, horseback riding. Cute names were all a part of it: Muffy or Binky, for example, for girls, and Skip or Trip for boys. Brand names such as Lacoste and Dockers got the prep seal of approval, and these companies made their clothes to suit the look.

Not all preppies want to grow up and succeed in a world of money and leisure sports. The preppy look, in some closets, gets mixed up with punk and goth. A neat plaid skirt worn over heavy, black goth boots, for example, would catch your eye. Fashion can be about drawing attention, and some people just like to mix up looks and confuse everyone else.

Punkin' Out

Punks wear jeans with studs and rips, cheap camouflage gear from the Army-Navy store, or skinny leather pants. They like T-shirts with obnoxious comments or the names of bands, fingerless gloves, and spiky hair in different colors. Jean jackets and fishnets are punky, too, along with lots of tattoos and piercings, Converse sneakers, and heavy black boots. Punk girls wear mascara and eyeshadow, while punk guys buy used black blazers and rip them to shreds, adding buttons or studs to grab your eye.

Punk rock started the punk style. It all began in London in the 1970s, when bands such as the Clash and the Sex Pistols were smashing guitars and acting out all over England. Punks had no money but didn't mind looking that way. A lot of them

The punk look includes piercings as well as spiky hair in
far-out colors.

Getting the Hang of Fashion and Dress Codes

just made their own clothes from stuff they found here or there. The music and the look crossed the Atlantic Ocean and showed up with the Ramones, famous for leather jackets and songs with a chord or two. Punk rock was loud and simple, and nothing like disco or mainstream FM rock.

Punk stars were famous all over the world for their strange behavior. In the punk world, acting out of it was very in. Anyway, it was tough to act normal with a tall green mohawk. When punk music started going out of style, punk fashion stayed in. The rebellion was over when stores that specialize in expensive punky clothes opened up. As punk fashion moved up into the mainstream (somewhat), fashion designers started using it in clothes for men and women. Punk clothes and accessories appeared in malls all over the United States.

Invasion of the Goths

One stream of punk rock had a dark feeling. The musicians wore black. Their music was depressing. They wore some heavy makeup, and they looked like death warmed over. Punk rock was sheer rebellion, while goth rock was pure Halloween.

Goth fans got into paganism, mythology, and the supernatural. They were dressed for a macabre funeral all the time. They used dark eyeliner, black lipstick, and painted their fingernails black. Spiked collars and wristbands, chains, and other gear went pretty well with the dark clothes, dyed hair, multiple piercings, and makeup.

There were all kinds of movies, music, and books joining the goth wave. Horror movies were always good, and so was Marilyn Manson and *The Nightmare Before Christmas*. Horror stories from the nineteenth century were seen as goth. Vampires were very goth, and the music and fashion style started up a whole new literary genre, the modern vampire novel.

Goth rock started to die out, but goth style survived along with the punk look. Dressing goth was a way to express drama and mystery. If you saw a goth, you couldn't ignore her or him. Best of all, it bugged the parents.

Hippies and Mods

Fashion always reacts against the past. In the 1960s, the past was going out of style and fast. The 1950s were all about conforming. There were a few gangs and dropouts and of course beatniks, with their jazz, poetry, and turtleneck shirts. But there wasn't much outlandish fashion going on. People were still striving to reach the middle class, dressing in conformity with others in their social and economic group.

The 1960s brought in the hippie, a new kind of rebel. Hippies dropped out of society and tried to live a new way. It was a reaction against middle-class conformity. Of course, hippies had their own fashion look, which was supposed to be nonfashionable. They intended to shock the older generation by dressing way, way out of style. Strangely, they all started to look alike.

All About Goth

Teens wearing black clothing and dark eyeshadow may not realize that the origins of goth style go back a couple of thousand years and tap into some of the most ancient fears of "civilized" Europeans. Not the fear of ghosts and goblins, or haunted mansions, or otherworldly denizens of the night; instead, a terror of very real people, specifically the Goths. They were a nomadic German tribe who invaded the western Roman Empire in the fifth century. Their migration, along with that of related tribes from the north, played an important role in destroying Roman institutions in Italy and other parts of western Europe. To the Romans, the Goths were real barbarians who couldn't speak decent Latin and dressed in animal skins and other crummy clothing as well. Their language wasn't worth writing down or even writing about, until a historian coined the term "Gothic" for it in 1611. Later on, in the Victorian era, "Gothic" came to be associated with everything primitive and medieval, and the gloomy Gothic novel played on superstitions and fears of the unknown.

Goth took punk to a new level, with spiked collars and wristbands, lots of chains, and black eyeliner—on guys as well as girls.

Prom Night

For most teens, it's never much fun to dress up because it usually means having to do something boring with adults. The exception to the rule is prom night. That's the night, one time a year, when teens get to put on something formal and fancy and then go out and dance.

Girls have to pick out a dress good for mingling, dancing, and showing off. It's supposed to be beautiful and romantic. Once upon a time there was a limited choice of colors and looks. Prom dresses were long and flouncy.

Nowadays prom-goers take their cues from movie and TV stars, who have their own formal kind of nights at awards shows such as the Academy Awards. The dresses that appear at this show, which happens early in the year, set the style for proms all over the country, which happen later in the spring. Way back in 2006, BusinessWire set out just a few of the models for that year's prom fashion:

> This year, a few looks that were worth imitating were Michelle Williams' canary yellow chiffon Vera Wang dress; Sandra Bullock's strapless blue Angel Sanchez; Jessica Alba's bronze, ornate Versace; Lindsay Lohan's stylish form-fitting Christian LaCroix gown, reminiscent of Tinseltown's golden-age sirens; and, finally, Jennifer Lopez's timeless and elegant chiffon Jean Desses gown.[1]

Prom has to be planned out well in advance. There are Web sites, magazine articles, and stores ready to give advice. The number of people that will go in your limo has to be secured so that you can put down a deposit. Girls have to think about dresses, shoes, hairstyles, and so on. The colors must complement hair color, skin tone, and eye color, and the fabric has to look and feel good. Many girls book appointments in salons to get their hair, makeup, and nails done for the big event. For boys, prom shopping is much simpler—a nice tuxedo with a vest or cummerbund and tie that go with his date's dress does just fine. You can just rent one, and bring it back the next day. It's good to be a guy sometimes.

What's Your Style?

And in London, mod clothes ruled (there were a lot of fashion trends starting up in London, it seems). The clothes were modern looking, of course. There were bright colors that didn't look quite natural, and strange materials, such as vinyl, used for jackets and skirts. Mod was all about fame and glamour. It was the opposite of hippie, even though it happened at the same time. Twiggy was a famous mod model, and the Who and the Beatles were the moddest of English bands.

Mod and hippie are still fighting it out. Tie-dye shirts and bell-bottom jeans are back in style, along with halter tops, low-lying belts, and miniskirts. (Some of these looks can get you into trouble at school, however.) Big round sunglasses and striped leggings are typical of mod style, as are knee-high boots and short hairstyles with heavy straight bangs that make you look like you're wearing a space helmet. Camouflage clothes come from hippie style. In the 1960s, they represented opposition to the military and against the Vietnam War. Nowadays camo shirts and pants are just a fashion statement.

Subcultural Fashion

There are a lot of fashion styles that don't quite fit a category. These style subcultures come and go. There is urban primitive, lounge culture (also known as "the cocktail way of life"), hipster, suburban retro, geek dress, punk holdouts, and so on. Some of these looks come from fads that turn into profitable, mass-market businesses. Skateboarding, for example, goes back a

few generations, but skateboard "culture" is definitely 1970s California, where a lot of new moves and new boards showed up. Some people got into skateboarding full-time, and went to exhibitions and competitions. Skateboarding got to be a lifestyle, like surfing. Skateboarders had some standard gear: skinny jeans, T-shirts with skateboard company logos, big shoes with rips and tears (to show how hard they ride their boards), and tilted baseball caps. Big hoodies are skater style, too. Shoulder-length, shaggy hair went with the skater look and meant that skaters concentrated on the skating and didn't really have time to waste making their hair look good, much less combed.

Lolita Fashion

Teenage girls in Japan love to follow trends, and one of the biggest is Lolita fashion. The look includes long dresses, frilly blouses, high-heeled shoes, white gloves, parasols, and hats. In Vladimir Nabokov's novel *Lolita,* a middle-aged college professor develops a romantic obsession with an adolescent girl. Lolita fashion is a way to express youthful innocence. It copies the fashion of England during the nineteenth century, known as the Victorian or Edwardian Eras, after a queen and a king of England. Lolita fashionistas study old photographs and movies to get their trend straight. Lolita is a way of rebelling against twentieth-century rebellion. It's a throwback to tradition, and a way of rejecting weird modern fashion that just wants to surprise or shock people.

Lolita fashion, popular in Japan, includes long, frilly dresses in Victorian or Edwardian style.

Some Lolita girls carry dolls or teddy bears as accessories. There are specialty shops that will dress girls up in Lolita style and of course conventions where Lolitas get together to have some fun. In this fashion trend, there are subcultures of the subculture: Lolita goths and punks, for example, who wear lacy black clothes and lots of makeup, and Wa Lolita, in which girls combine the Lolita look with kimonos and other traditional Japanese gear. The Lolita guy is a *ouji*, "prince," and he puts on knee-length trousers and suit jackets, and sometimes wears old-fashioned bowler hats or top hats.

Lolita fashion isn't catching on yet in the United States or Europe. For one thing, there aren't models to set the trend— no rock stars or movie stars in the West dressing

Getting the Hang of Fashion and Dress Codes

up in old Victorian fashions. Second, there aren't too many stores that carry the clothes and the gear. But throughout the United States, Japanese manga and anime have a huge audience. Many of the characters in these stories dress Lolita style, and in this way, show the audience how it's done.

Steampunk

It looks a lot different, but the closest thing to Lolita fashion in these parts is steampunk: fashion and style from the time when steam power was key. Steampunk is an obsession with objects and gadgets from the Victorian age, combined with a punk attitude toward the world at large. Girls wear petticoats and lacy blouses (sometimes made with leather), while guys wear nice dark-colored jackets, vests, suspenders, and boots. Steampunkers love accessories such as goggles, walking sticks, and pocket watches. These objects don't always have to be old-fashioned. Modern gear such as cell phones and computers can be dressed up with the look by being set in an ornate brass or iron frame. One of the hottest steampunk accessories is a weird-looking ray gun toy that might come straight from the prop closet of a 1950s science fiction movie set.

Steampunk pairs clothing from the Victorian era with modern technology (such as computers and cell phones) made to look old-fashioned.

Goths and punks love steampunk because it's an antifashion fashion. There's not much that fancy designer labels such as Calvin Klein and Gucci can do about steampunk—the clothes are expensive to make and don't have a large market, and fashion designers don't like working in retro styles that don't allow them to set any new trends. Steampunk and other fashion subcultures have this in common: a bad attitude toward marketing and fashion trends in general.

Getting the Hang of Fashion and Dress Codes

Boys, Girls, Teenagers, and Marketing

Fashion has a way of emphasizing differences in gender, race, economic class, and social status. Teens deal with guidance and instructions offered by parents, family, friends, and teachers. Each morning a decision must be reached on the clothing they wear and the statement it will make.

Boys and girls have generally different attitudes toward dress. Generally, but with many exceptions, girls are keenly aware of the social ladder. They're also more fashion conscious. Females are often stereotyped as being obsessed with buying new purses and shoes. Boys, on the other hand, stand more independent from trends. Sometimes they don't care what they wear. As the English author Anthony Burgess said, "Women thrive on novelty and are easy meat for the commerce of fashion. Men prefer old pipes and torn jackets."[1] There are stereotypes that most people feel they should conform to.

Boys

- feel a keen sense of physical competition with other boys;

- want to be tough and strong;

- like to win, hate to lose;

- don't show their emotions much;

- are never supposed to cry;

- can show anger at times.

The stereotypical girl, on the other hand, is

- geared more toward cooperation than competition;

- likes to make emotional bonds with friends;

- feels pressure to be cooperative with adults;

Getting the Hang of Fashion and Dress Codes

- has a keen sense of her place on the social ladder;

  doesn't like to fight, although many girls enjoy competing in sports or other pursuits.

These basic gender roles have changed over time and vary from one culture to the next. A big part of being a teenager is defying these stereotypes and the rules that everyone else has set out for teens to follow. Still, as everyone knows, "The clothes you wear, how and whether you use makeup or jewelry, and the activities you choose in and out of school send signals to the rest of the world about your gender role. They fit society's image of being either masculine or feminine."[2]

The First Cool Guys: Teddy Boys

In England, before there were mods and rockers, there were teddy boys. This trend began in the 1950s. In those years young men had to do "national service," meaning they had to spend some time in the military. They had to wear uniforms even while off duty, which was fine, because the heroes of the time were veterans who had fought in World War II.

Teddy boys broke away from the norm and created their own uniform—tight trousers, suit jackets, and narrow ties.

The teddy boys were working-class guys who broke away from the social norms and put together their own uniform. Their fathers were poorly dressed because there wasn't much money, and during the war nobody was buying nice new clothes. The teddy boys wanted to look smart and slick. They wore narrow trousers and long suit jackets, sometimes trimmed with velvet, that fell all the way to the knees. The jackets had several pockets, narrow lapels, and big cuffs that rode above the hand. Teddy boys wore narrow ties and sometimes string ties that looked like shoelaces. They slicked their hair back and combed it to a point in the back that resembled a ducktail.

Many young men in fashionable London and other English cities followed the teddy boy trend for about a decade, until the mods and rockers came along. It was a way for them to join a group and have some kind of identity, outside of "working class." An outfit gave them some respect among outsiders, and it hid their status as poorly paid laborers or office workers.

The teddy boy didn't travel too well across the Atlantic to the United States, where long suit jackets never quite caught on (unless one really wanted to look English). But there were certain style icons in the United States as well, including bikers, beatniks, and "dudes," meaning guys with white socks, white shoes, pleated trousers, and jackets with five buttons down the front.

Bobby-soxers were the postwar girl icon in the United States. They were big fans of Frank Sinatra, who crooned gently into the microphone while his swooning audience

The styles of the 1950s included sweaters, slacks, and sneakers for boys, and sweaters with skirts and saddle shoes with bobby sox for girls.

watched and dreamed. They wore white socks that came in style during World War II, when they couldn't buy nylon or silk for stockings. The ankle socks came from England, where policemen were called "bobbies."

The bobby-soxer was a rebel, at first, because she didn't dress like her mother. But soon the look went mainstream. It was all in the socks, which had to show one way or the other.

Getting the Hang of Fashion and Dress Codes

If a girl wore pants, she had to pull the cuffs up. If the socks were long, she had to fold them down (bobby sox had to be short—too far above the ankle wasn't good).

Girls wore saddle shoes and their good white socks to school dances. But most schools made students take off their leather shoes if they wanted to dance. That way, the polished wood of the gym floor wouldn't get scuffed. So dances got to be known as sock hops.

The fashion trends of mods, rockers, bobby-soxers, and teddy boys all came from the ordinary people who adopted the styles of their peers. They just put on the clothes they wanted to be seen in and picked up on trends. The trend came and went as these ordinary people got bored with old things and tried something new. There's a big difference in fashion trends and style nowadays. Many twenty-first-century trends arise out of marketing campaigns, which are created in the offices of large companies. They are business strategies, designed to make money.

The New Cool

Fashion changes fast, and especially fast since an international mass audience developed for images and style. By the 1990s, mods, rockers, and hippies were out. The clothing industry and the media had to come up with some kind of new icon on which they could model characters seen in movies, on TV, and in advertisements.

A 2001 television documentary, "The Merchants of Cool," had a label for the modern boy/girl icons: "mooks" and "midriffs." The mook was a guy who was pretty casual about what he wore. He didn't take the world seriously at all. He wasn't too smart, he watched a lot of TV, he was into cars and sports, and he ran in a pack of friends who all looked and acted very much the same.

Host Douglas Rushkoff defined the mook: "You can find him almost any hour of the day or night somewhere on MTV. He's not real. He's a character—crude, loud, obnoxious, and in-your-face. . . . He's Tom Green of The Tom Green Show . . . . He's those frat boys and their whip-cream bikini girlfriends on MTV's constantly recurring Spring Break specials . . . . He has migrated to MTV's sister network, Comedy Central, where he's the cartoon cutouts of South Park or the lads on The Man Show."[3]

The midriff was Britney Spears, wearing low-rider jeans and a halter top. This midriff followed the trends like a slave. She did her best to look good and spent a lot of money at the mall.

During the early twenty-first century, Britney Spears was a favorite star with girls just getting into their teens and into fashion. Clothing companies ramped up their marketing efforts to these customers. They started designing fashion for the "tween" girl, who didn't yet know that she wanted low-rise jeans, high-cut shirts, bikinis, glitter eye shadow, pedicure kits, and fake nails. People in the industry were just doing their jobs: "This has been the trend for quite some time in girls sizes 7 to 14," said one member of the Fashion Institute of Technology in New York. "It started with the Spice Girls and Britney Spears. The girls watch the entertainers and they

Getting the Hang of Fashion and Dress Codes

want to mimic them. It is not for the industry to say you should be wearing this. We produce what our market would like to wear."[4]

The boy/girl icons serve the clothing industry by showing customers what they should be aspiring to. It's the point of advertising to make you come up short. In the book *Boy v. Girl?* George Abrahams and Sheila Ahlbrand describe the strategy: "In order to want to buy something, you have to feel like you need it. You need to feel like there's something in your life that will be missing if you can't have that particular product. You have to feel like you're not good enough, not pretty or handsome enough, not cool enough."[5]

No market is better for this kind of approach than teenagers, who work hard to define themselves, and who always feel like they're not quite measuring up to the expectations of parents, teachers, and friends.

Boys, Girls, Teenagers, and Marketing

Marlon Brando (right) in *The Wild One* and James Dean (above) in *Rebel Without a Cause* showed the coolest ways to act and dress.

Getting the Hang of Fashion and Dress Codes

How Trends Happen

Little known to most people, teenagers were invented in 1950. Before that time, children were born and just stayed children until they were suddenly off to work, or reached adulthood. They went to school, lived at home, dressed in clothes their parents gave them, and then left school, got married, and turned into adults. Many kids didn't spend much time in classrooms at all, as their families needed them to make money. Clothes for kids weren't much different from clothes for adults, just smaller. Young boys wore short pants until puberty, when they graduated to long trousers. Young girls wore dresses or blouses and skirts.

World War II ended in 1945. There were big changes in England and the United States. People had some money to spend. They could afford better clothes. They could go out to movies, or stay at home and watch the new entertainment device—television. People, young and old, watched TV and movies for clues about the coolest way to dress. *The Wild One* came out in 1953 with Marlon Brando, and *Rebel Without a Cause* a few years later starred James Dean. Brando played an out-of-control biker who wore leather jackets and caused a lot of turmoil and trouble in small towns. James Dean played a young guy who defied all the rules of parents, adults, family, and society. The jean-wearing bad boys from both films were every teenager's dream and every parent's nightmare.

Clothing and media companies discovered a big new group of customers: teenagers. They made clothes and entertainment for this audience and showed them how to be different from their parents and the older generation. Old fashion trends came from the appearance of the wealthy, of those people who could afford tailored and expensive clothes. New trends came from rebellious young people who just wanted a different look.

Teenagers came on strong through the 1960s and 1970s with the hippie look, rock and roll, and dropping out—of jobs, gender roles, and the middle class. Rebellion against the rules came to define the fashion trend. Punk and grunge upset parents through the 1980s, and then "retro" looks and preppy started offending punks in the 1990s. Emo, steampunk, goth, and hipster came along, each trying hard to stand out.

How to Market

Six teenagers sit around a conference table in comfortable chairs. A marketing expert says hello and starts asking them questions about what they like to do, where they like to go, what their friends like, what kind of clothes they wear, what shoes look good. Then he shows them a board with a dozen brand logos and asks them to circle the ones they like and cross out the ones they don't. He turns on a television monitor and clicks through the images of sports stars, movie actors, and fashion models. He asks more questions about what they're seeing, and takes lots of notes.

The focus group is the way to find out what teenagers think is cool. It's basic market research that takes place every day. Big companies pay consultants to find out the next wave of fashion, so they can make some products in that style and catch the wave early. If they can hit a trend just right—meaning just before it goes mass market—they can make tons of money.

Selling Stuff

The marketing and advertising industries are pretty good at what they do. For at least a century, advertisers have relied on the natural human desire to be respected and loved. They employ this desire in order to sell products such as clothing, shoes, appliances, and cars. They have always appealed to an individual's sense of worthiness, gauged by what he or she owns. Under the influence of print, radio, and television advertising, people came to associate the good life with possessions, and this point was underlined by the appearance of happy people accompanied by nice things.

Boys, Girls, Teenagers, and Marketing

During this distant past (before the 1970s), stores sold clothing by its material; the more expensive the basic material, the more expensive and prestigious the clothing. A pair of trousers or a blouse came from Montgomery Ward or Sears or the local tailor. Clothing manufacturers were nearly invisible companies that produced the stuff and marketed it through wholesalers (also invisible). Then brand names and designer labels became an important part of the fashion industry.

The marketing industry went through a big change by the time the 1960s were over. The target audience changed again in the 1990s, becoming younger. The baby boomers—people born in the generation following World War II—started going out of style. For the first time in many years, the number of teenagers, the daughters and sons of the baby boomers, started to rise. The most successful consumer-products companies were catering to a younger market, teenagers and young adults. This was the market for new fast-food restaurants, movies, soft drinks, and clothing. This was the demographic spending more and more money for the cachet of prestigious brand names and designer labels.

The Strategy

For a long time, marketing strategy has used two simple steps: 1. identify a need and 2. promise to fulfill it. The idea is to make people want something and convince them that getting whatever it is they want will make them happy. Step one

In the 1990s, the marketing industry began targeting younger people as the number of teenagers rose.

Boys, Girls, Teenagers, and Marketing

is achieved when images of beauty, wealth, and glamour are shown in a television commercial or a magazine ad. The images cause the targets to compare themselves to the people in the ads and find themselves not measuring up. The implication is that the product will put them in the same clothes, the same car, the same expensive house as the people pictured and that the same glamour and success will follow.

Fashion and the marketing business were made for each other, as author Stephen Bayle explained in his book *Taste:* "Fashion is the most intense expression of the phenomenon of neomania [passion for the new], which  has grown ever since the birth of capitalism. Neomania assumes that purchasing the new is the same as acquiring value. . . . If the purchase of a new garment coincides with the wearing out of an old one, then obviously there is no fashion. . . . Fashion flourishes on surplus, when someone buys more than he or she needs."[6]

Trends don't last long. A certain cut or shape or color can be in style this year, out the next. This gives the marketing company plenty to do. Each season needs a new approach, a new look. In the year 2000, it was flared jeans or parachute pants, with pockets and zippers.

Getting the Hang of Fashion and Dress Codes

Camouflage pants came in the next year, and in 2003 it was miniskirts. Each trend alters a look seen before and gives it a new twist that makes it a novelty and, with luck and marketing skill, a hot fashion.

Starting Young

Brand-name marketing begins with the very young. Toddlers watching television want certain action figures, such as Superman and Batman, or certain character dolls, such as Barbie, Dora, or Tickle Me Elmo. When they grow older, they learn to favor certain brands. They develop loyalty to the brands they know best in breakfast cereals, candy bars, toys, games, and shoes. At first, brand loyalty is a personal thing. As kids socialize with others, they form groups of friends that share interests and an identity. They place themselves within the group by following what the others are doing or wearing.

As they grow up, children gain loyalties to brands designed for older kids and teenagers. Using movies and television, shoe and clothing companies expose their styles by having stars use them or wear them. These endorsements can be worth a lot of money. In 2001, Nike paid Tiger Woods $105 million just to wear visors and shirts with the company logo, and to appear in Nike advertising, for the next five years. In the movies, companies buy the rights to have their products seen for a few seconds on the screen. By providing money, these product placement deals help movies get made, and they help companies sell their stuff.

By the time customers reach the age of eighteen, they or their parents have bought thousands of dollars worth of books, games, and name-brand clothing, shoes, and accessories. They've been looking at advertising messages every day. For every single one, they formed an opinion, good or bad. The messages and ads just keep coming, on TV, by the side of the road, on the side of the bus, in magazines, on the Internet, before the movie begins, and inside the store.

Clothing retailers depend on the fact that fashions constantly go in and out of style. If one style held on for years and years, then people would not need to buy new clothes so often. The turnover in fashion means high turnover in the store and a profitable business.

The Cool Factor

Cool clothes are a big part of it. Your average teenager wants to fit in with the rest, to appear fashionable, at the cutting edge. Nobody wants to be un-chic, dorky, or nerdy (outside of geeksters who have their own un-chic look and wear it proudly). Media and clothing companies know all about this. They want to be famous for having the coolest stuff, making and selling as much of it as possible, and earning lots of money. They have to work hard to find out what's cool because there aren't very many really cool people around. By definition, cool is something hard to find, rare, and just this side of weird.

A Market for Stories

The Abercrombie & Fitch company may not know much about history, but they know how to market clothing. In their view, it takes more than a certain style or color, matched to the season and to popular taste, to inspire shoppers to buy. It takes a great, convincing backstory.

The Ruehl 925 line was targeted to young adults who went to college. This clothing dated back to the Ruehls, German immigrants who moved to Greenwich Village in New York and sold leather goods. Their descendants sold blue jeans and other gear to the hippest hippies in the Village and, in 2002, Abercrombie bought the family business.

Gilly Hicks was an English designer who moved to a swanky neighborhood in Sydney, Australia, where she started a business in 1932 to make clothes for fashionable ladies.

Her customers loved the comfort and elegant look of her blouses and bras, which reminded them of proper Victorian times.

John Hollister was an athletic preppy from New England who ventured to the East Indies, where he bought a rubber plantation. He sailed across the Pacific with his love, Meta, finally anchoring in Los Angeles and starting a company in 1922 to sell crafts, jewelry, and clothes from Polynesia. His son, John Jr., an expert surfer, carried on the family business as a hip and trendy surf shop; the Hollister brand now lives on in apparel, shoes, and other gear made just for cool teenagers.

All three stories are just that: stories. Abercrombie & Fitch made them up and uses them to market clothing, trying to match each character and story to the desires and dreams of a specific market segment. Remember: the next time you wear Hollister or any other Abercrombie brand, you're wearing a good story, and not just a designer label.

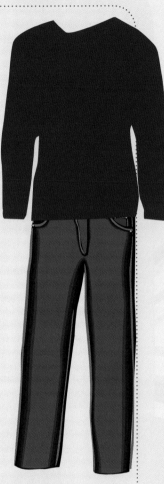

The fashion industry even has a word for it: the coolhunt. This means looking for the new thing, whatever it may be, in shoes and clothes. There are specialists and experts in coolhunting, and there's a whole big business of consultants who promise to find it fast, for a fee. There are Web sites devoted to it, such as coolhunt.net, and there are writers who write about it for newspapers and fashion magazines. Malcolm Gladwell discovered the coolhunt for the *New Yorker* magazine in 1997, and wrote:

> It's now about chase and flight—designers and
> retailers and the mass consumer giving chase to
> the elusive prey of street cool. . . . The sneakers of
> Nike and Reebok used to come out yearly. Now a
> new style comes out every season. Apparel
> designers used to have an eighteen-month lead
> time between concept and sale. Now they're
> reducing that to a year, or even six months, in
> order to react faster to new ideas from the
> street. . . . [T]he better coolhunters become at
> bringing the mainstream close to the cutting edge,
> the more elusive the cutting edge becomes. This is
> the first rule of the cool: The quicker the chase, the
> quicker the flight. The act of discovering what's
> cool is what causes cool to move on.[7]

Not everyone is happy about the way media and clothing companies work together to sell fashion to young people. Some oppose the consumer culture, the pressure to constantly spend

Clothing retailers market their merchandise through constant advertising, developing brand-name loyalty among their customers over time.

86

Getting the Hang of Fashion and Dress Codes

money on fashion, and the images the media creates to sell an image and its products. They don't like marketing to younger children, especially girls, and the way marketers and retailers try to make girls into women by selling them sexy clothes and even makeup. Some people find the whole system a sign of a whole civilization going bad. Walter Schneider said as much on the Web site Fathers for Life:

> To claim that the media deliberately corrupt society may seem a little strong. However, it matters little what words are chosen to describe the process of culturing the basest instincts of young children, teenagers and young adults—all for nothing more than to make a profit.[8]

Maybe so, but in an economy based on free enterprise, competition, and the profit motive, companies will do whatever it takes to succeed. The clothing business is all about pleasing the customer, catching his or her eye, and tempting him or her to spend. It's just a big business that simply uses the surrounding culture, and its taste for money, fame, and fashion, to do its job.

Chapter 6 Rag Trades

After a long trip, new clothing finally arrives at the mall store, ready for you to try on. A huge fashion and retail clothing industry brought it to the store, to the racks, and finally into your closet. But it all begins in the head of a professional fashion designer.

As shown on the television show *Project Runway*, designers go through a complex process in creating clothing: choosing fabric, designing a pattern, sewing the pieces together, and fitting the garment.

89

Rag Trades

Designers can either freelance or work "in-house," meaning they go to an office every day and get a regular paycheck. They have trained for the business in small fashion schools, they've apprenticed to an experienced designer, or they've spent some time in low-level jobs with a fashion company. Once they earn the title of fashion designer, they work through a long and complex process to create new clothes. They sketch out the cut, texture, color, and "drape"—how the clothing curves and falls. To decide on the right material, they use small swatches of fabric provided by textile makers. They are designing for a season and using colors and fabrics that are in style. There might be a new color that's popular, or a new weave that has a different feel and look from fabric that has come before.

Getting the Hang of Fashion and Dress Codes

Designers have a good idea, from reading, fashion shows, and the media, of what's going to do well in the retail market. The company they work for has a certain look and style, which they know well. The hot style, of course, is always changing. The best designers have a good feel for this market, and they always think ahead.

The finished design goes to a pattern maker. This person creates a heavy paper card that shows the precise measurements of the pieces that go into the garment. The pattern card can then be sent to a factory, where it is used as a blueprint for a finished piece of clothing. The factory creates a few samples, which then travel to a fashion show.

Fashion shows take place in the world's fashion capitals: New York, Paris, Milan, or Tokyo. Models put on the new clothes, and stroll up and down a catwalk while music blares, photographers shoot, and writers take notes. Backstage, designers, hairstylists, and makeup artists rush about as the models dress and prepare.

Professional buyers for retail chains such as the Gap, Banana Republic, and Saks Fifth Avenue watch the show carefully. The photographs and stories appear in magazines such as *Vogue*, *GQ*, and *Elle*. A marketing campaign begins, and the new clothing appears in print ads. Finally the clothes are mass-produced and shipped to retail stores. Designers and clothing makers are already looking ahead to the next season.

Different Money, Different Markets

In earlier times, people with money had their clothes made by tailors and seamstresses. These specialists took careful measurements to get the fit just right. They used wool and cotton, spun in certain weights and dyed natural colors. A few customers—not many—still have their clothes made to order. Ready-to-wear clothes can fit and look just as good.

Ready-to-wear is a fashion market that began in the middle of the twentieth century. Manufacturers use the latest designs and good material, but they don't make clothes for individual customers. Instead, the clothing comes in standard sizes, one of which will fit the standard-sized person. Twice a year, fashion companies come out with new collections.

The mass-market fashion industry caters to ordinary people who don't have a lot of money to spend on clothes. The companies that serve this market follow the trends, but they don't set them. They sell their clothing through big stores, with a big selection of every kind of clothing in all the standard sizes. They need high turnover, meaning they have to move as much as they can from the back room to the cash register and out the door. The profit margin on mass-market clothing is low, and the costs of running a store are high. And if the customers don't like the clothes much, they can just walk a very short distance to the next store for a look at something else.

Getting the Hang of Fashion and Dress Codes

The Clothing Factory

The competition in this industry is intense. Most of the designers, clothing makers, and retailers need to keep their costs down. They don't have large budgets to pay workers better, buy better fabric, or use heavier stitching that will hold the clothes together longer. They manufacture the clothing overseas because that's where wages are lowest, and that's where every other company in the same business is making its clothes and shoes.

In order to make a profit, expenses must be controlled. Mass-market clothing companies don't spend much on original design or high-priced fabrics. They set up factories in Asia—China, Malaysia, and Bangladesh, for example, have thousands of factories where clothing and shoes are made. Other clothing factories are operating in Central America and Mexico. Big retail chains such as Wal-Mart can set the price they will pay a factory for clothing. In some cases, Wal-Mart is the only buyer for the goods a factory makes. Wal-Mart needs its products to be as cheap as possible. If a factory tries to charge the company more, or if its costs rise, chances are good that it will lose the Wal-Mart contract, and then go out of business.

The workers in clothing factories have simple, repetitive jobs. Some move around bolts of fabric and bales of yarn. Others sit at small tables and use sewing machines that stitch together precut pieces of cheaply bought fabric. The clothing factory works like a car factory, where everyone has a specific

To save on costs, makers of mass-market clothing set up their manufacturing operations overseas. Here is a clothing factory in India.

Getting the Hang of Fashion and Dress Codes

job to do: sewing pockets, for example, or applying zippers or buttons. The workers make very little per hour. Many are very young, and most are female and unmarried. Factory owners prefer to hire women, as they have smaller, more nimble hands and generally give less trouble than men. In China and other countries, there's no law against discriminating against workers on the basis of their gender. There is also no minimum wage.

Some workers turn out clothing on the piecework system. When doing piecework, a worker earns a set amount for each item he or she produces. The faster they can do the work, the more money they can earn. Under this system, many workers don't earn any kind of benefit, such as health insurance, vacations, sick time, or pensions. They work out of their homes, and they don't earn anything for working overtime or on holidays.

Some clothing factories pay workers poorly and force them to work long hours in crowded, unhealthy conditions. The workers have little say in the matter, as they are not allowed to organize themselves or form unions to demand changes. Labor laws in many foreign countries are weak or nonexistent. One clothing factory in Guatemala, owned by a Korean company named Fribo, cheated its workers in another way, as reported by the *Milwaukee Journal Sentinel* in 2007: "Fribo has deducted payments for Social Security from workers' paychecks but has not paid the money to the government, as is required by law. This results in the loss of health care and pensions for the workers."[1]

Workers complained about the cheating and the poor conditions to a nonprofit group in Guatemala, which then reported to the National Labor Committee in New York. When the word got out to the press, the scandal touched Kohl's, a big American retailer. Through a vendor known as P.A. Group, Kohl's had women's blouses made at the factory. The tops carried the Daisy Fuentes label. As the scandal spread, four companies were now involved: the factory owner, the clothing vendor, the designer, and the retailer.

In order to keep their costs down, and make a profit, clothing retailers have their clothes made cheap. They hire manufacturers who use "sweatshops" in poor countries, such as Guatemala, where people desperately need jobs to feed and support their families. The Fribo company paid its workers twenty-five cents for each blouse they made. When the blouses finally made it to the Kohl's stores in the United States, they were selling for $22 to $38.[2]

No company wants the bad publicity that comes with news reports of sweatshop conditions. Of course, if they decide to cancel their contracts, the factory might have to lay off workers,

Getting the Hang of Fashion and Dress Codes

A woman in Guatemala sews pants. Sweatshops—factories in which people work in poor conditions for little pay—are a problem in many Central American countries.

who might find themselves out of a job permanently, in a place where even poorly paid jobs are hard to find. "The worst thing that . . . Kohl's management could do," wrote Charles Kernaghan of the National Labor Committee to Daisy Fuentes, "is to 'cut and run,' pulling your work from the Fribo factory, which would only further punish these workers, who have already suffered a great deal. The workers and their children desperately need and depend upon these jobs for their survival."[3]

In the Fribo case, Kohl's canceled some production at the factory. They then demanded that Fribo improve conditions for its workers. Fribo signed an agreement that it would adhere to "Western" standards in its factories. It would transfer the money for pension and health benefits to the government of Guatemala instead of keeping the money. The workers would have the benefits they were paying for. They would be paid for overtime work. The owner of the factory has also agreed to weekly inspections of the facility in order to guarantee that it complies with the law.

Many other companies have dealt with scandals over how their clothes and shoes are made. Fashion retailers understand that bad publicity about sweatshops can hurt their sales and profits. Most of them have

Getting the Hang of Fashion and Dress Codes

agreements with vendors and factory owners about the pay and treatment of workers. Organizations such as United Students Against Sweatshops and the National Labor Committee keep an eye on factories, set down guidelines, make inspections, keep contact with workers, and attempt to improve working conditions in clothing factories in the United States and abroad.

Watch Out! Counterfeit!

Organized criminal gangs make billions from selling counterfeit clothes. They fake the labels and designs and run sweatshops all over the world to turn out the fakes. Because retail stores only buy direct from manufacturers and legitimate wholesalers, this big business needs an outlet. The Internet is a favorite spot, as no government can completely control it. If you want to buy the real thing, watch out for Internet sites. One way to tell is to look for a disclaimer on the Web page about the Internet Privacy Act of 1995, supposedly signed by President Bill Clinton. If the Web page claims it follows this law, then it's up to no good, because the Internet Privacy Act doesn't exist. Many clothing counterfeiters have been caught and shut down this way.

Green Clothing

A small but growing number of clothing companies are going green. This means not harming the environment while manufacturing or selling clothes. "Green" clothing is made from natural fibers, such as cotton, that are grown without pesticides that poison soil and water. Green factories use nonpolluting sources of energy such as solar power, hydropower, or geothermal power (which comes from underground steam and heat). Green fashion can be made from recycled material, such as old clothes that are washed, chopped up, mashed together, and woven again into clean, new fabric. Even plastic bottles can be recycled into shoes and clothing. The greenest fashion is the clothing you already have in your closet—wearing it means no expense, waste, or environmental damage is involved.

You can clean green as well, by buying clothes you don't need to wash in hot water or—the worst—have dry-cleaned (too many nasty chemicals used). The greenest laundry cycle is done in cold water, which uses less energy. Dryers are not environmentally friendly, as they require power that comes, in many communities, from the burning of coal. It's much greener to hang your clothes out on the line, as everyone did before the invention of clothes dryers.

Getting the Hang of Fashion and Dress Codes

The green way to use clothing is to buy less of it and make it last longer. The best way to do this is to be careful while choosing clothes, and to buy styles and colors that will still be stylish in a few years. It's not so easy, as clothing and marketing companies are seeing to it that styles and coolness change constantly.

Businesses in the clothing industry are careful about their image because image is central to fashion. They want to appear green and to take some interest in working conditions in factories that make their products. But the industry probably won't support a ban on shopping anytime soon. It can't survive without constantly changing fashion trends and customers who seek them out.

Stitching the Label

Mass-market clothing companies deal with large chain stores, such as Wal-Mart, JC Penney, Sears, and Target. They meet with buyers from these companies. The buyers know their customers. They need their clothing to be made for a certain market and in a certain price range. Buyers and manufacturers negotiate the price for huge lots of clothing. The finished clothing travels from the factories to the retail stores in cargo container ships, then by trucks.

Clothing retailers take care to make sure their clothes have prestige. A label stating "Made in China" or "Made in Bangladesh" doesn't carry much prestige. By definition, fashionable clothes can't be ordinary. By law, however, the label that tells where the product was made has to tell the truth—at least part of the truth. For that reason, some companies have a small part of the item made in a European country, such as Italy, where wages are higher but where the reputation for making fine clothing is high as well.

The fanciest labels in the world, such as Prada and Gucci, still operate factories in Italy. They use Chinese immigrants to make their clothing, shoes, handbags, and scarves. The working conditions aren't good. Many workers sleep in the same factories where they work—house prices and apartment rents in Italy are expensive. There are thousands of small factories on the outskirts of Italian cities such as Naples and Florence. Inside, the workers make the same clothing, using the same

fabric and machinery, that they would have made in China. The only difference is the small white label they sew into the clothes reads "Made in Italy."

Using immigrant labor helps designer labels compete, but it also causes problems. Many Italian cities now have entire neighborhoods of poor immigrants who work in clothing factories. They also have thousands of factories making counterfeit articles that carry an easily made, fake designer label. The police raid these factories all the time. The owners close them down, then open another one nearby, hiring the same workers to do the same counterfeiting. The market in fake goods, sold on streets and in public markets all over the world, is just about as big as the market in legal clothing. It all depends on the worldwide demand for fashion.

Chapter 7 The Dreaded Dress Code

It's Day One at school, and the hall parade has just begun. Before the first bell rings, students shout and lockers clang. Teachers wait in their rooms, glancing at the desks and chalkboards to make sure all is in order. The time for the first class is fast approaching. Outside in the halls, a vast crowd mills about, carrying books and chatting at high volume. In the meantime, everyone is checking you out.

First thing in the morning was Decision Time. The bedroom closet didn't give much hope. There's a lot of forbidden stuff in there. Your torn jeans—no. Your halter top—no

Getting the Hang of Fashion and Dress Codes

way. The mildly obscene T-shirt—unh-unh. The camo gear, *verboten*. The sandals or the flip-flops, kind of trendy and so comfortable, but *no*.

Your local school board has a dress code, of course, and it's the school's job to enforce it. The code is the first thing they hand out or mail out every year. They want to keep order and discipline, and a sense that the students are all in this together. They don't want disruptions or distractions. So watch what you wear!

Whose Idea Was This, Anyway?

Dress codes go way back. In ancient Rome, only the emperor could wear the color purple. Slaves wore certain raggedy clothes and could wear no other. In medieval times, the kings (and queens) handed down sumptuary laws. The laws said what people could wear and what they couldn't—or else.

Clothing was supposed to mark out certain trades and social ranks. Everyone had his place on the social ladder. People didn't go up or down. Mingling of the classes was confusing and just a very dangerous idea, or so it was thought.

In England, at the time of Henry VIII, only the king and his family could wear clothes trimmed with ermine (the fur of a little white weasel). Nobles could wear lesser-grade furs such as fox, marten, and otter.

The sumptuary laws protected the realm from trouble and turmoil. The sheriff and his constables had enough to deal with, and as everyone knew, styling in totally top-rank threads eventually brought crime, delinquency, and the undoing of young gentlemen. As Queen Elizabeth put it so succinctly in her *Statutes of Apparel* in 1574:

> The excess of apparel and the superfluity of unnecessary foreign wares thereto belonging now of late years is grown by sufferance to such an extremity that the manifest decay of the whole realm generally is like to follow . . . but also particularly the wasting and undoing of a great number of young gentlemen, otherwise serviceable, and others seeking by show of apparel to be esteemed as gentlemen, who, allured by the vain show of those things, do not only consume themselves, their goods, and lands which their parents left unto them, but also run into such debts and shifts as they cannot live out of danger of laws without attempting unlawful acts, whereby they are not any ways serviceable to their country as otherwise they might be.[1]

Sumptuary laws continued for a few centuries before gradually dying out. Revolutions took place and members of the nobility began to lose their ancient privileges. In the nineteenth century, as incomes rose and factories started mass-producing clothes, nice stuff to wear got cheaper. The social classes began to mix more freely, and eventually opportunities for social mobility arrived. But school dress codes lived on.

Getting the Hang of Fashion and Dress Codes

Queen Elizabeth I put out her *Statutes of Apparel* in 1574, setting down standards for dress.

I Have to Wear *What?*

Schools throughout the world have uniforms—a standard, limited outfit that everyone must wear. Some uniform codes are strict, indeed. The usual outfit for boys has them in dark trousers, white or light-blue button-down shirts, formal shoes, and a tie. This is the prep school uniform that was common in England and then traveled to the United States about a century ago. Girls wear jumpers or skirts to the knee and a light-colored blouse.

The uniform varies with culture and climate. In cold places, some schools use uniform jackets. In Canada, all the Catholic schools have uniforms (public schools do not). In Japan, many kids in primary and junior high wear sailor suits. This getup dates back to the mid- to late-nineteenth century. Back then, Japan was imitating Western countries. As a sign of progress, they had their soldiers and sailors wear military uniforms after the fashion in the United States and Britain. These days most Japanese schools, private and public, have some kind of uniform. Each school has its distinctive look.

In Israel, where the weather is hot during the summer, schools want their students to wear a T-shirt that carries the school logo. The idea, as in many other countries, is to get rid of the different social and economic classes, and pull the population more closely together. For this reason, Israelis favor uniforms in school, and even some communities have a standard dress or shirt for people to wear.

In Germany, student hats came into fashion in the nineteenth century. Every different university had its own hat, some of them colorful and strange looking. Then the Nazi party came along in the 1930s. The Nazis banned the different school outfits and hats. Everyone was supposed to think about loyalty to the country and the government, first and foremost. Work, school, and family came next. The Hitler Youth was a group of young people training for membership in the Nazi party and service in the military. This group set down strict uniform requirements for its members.

In the Soviet Union, the All-Union Leninist Communist Union of Youth, also known as the Komsomol, was a youth group that prepared future leaders of the Communist party. Members wore bright red scarves.

In Italy uniforms were dropped after World War II as a reminder of the fascist era, but girls were still required to wear a smocklike garment known as a *grembiule*. The idea was not to distract the boys. But many women pointed out that this was a form of discrimination. It wasn't fair to make girls wear a specific article of clothing and not do the same to boys. The grembiule went out of use during the 1970s. But many primary school girls still wear the grembiule. Some people still want to go back to the grembiule. It's getting to be a hot topic in Italy.

A Muslim girl wears a traditional head scarf, or hijab. Some societies require head scarves; others prohibit them in public settings, such as schools.

Getting the Hang of Fashion and Dress Codes

Some Muslim societies have a strict code of dress for women, who must conform all their lives. In Afghanistan, the burqa completely conceals a woman's body and face. In Malaysia, Muslim girls wear a baju kurung, a tunic, and the hijab. This outfit is strictly enforced in Malaysian schools, and violators are sent home or subject to a beating with a cane. In Europe, where the Muslim community is growing as immigrants arrive from North Africa, the Middle East, and Turkey, these dress codes are generally left behind, with only the traditional head scarf remaining.

The wearing of head scarves in schools has become a hot political topic in France. The government has banned head scarves, also known as a hijab, claiming that it does not want to see a division among students along religious lines. France also prohibits religious symbols and signs by students in the public schools. Students can't wear a crucifix or a Star of David to school, or show them on their clothes in any way. As in many French things, it all goes back to the French Revolution and Napoléon. French leaders saw the church as opposed to the state.

The Dreaded Dress Code

In modern France, like in the United States, there is a separation of church and state. The church is kept away from public institutions of any kind, and especially schools.

Dress Codes in the United States

In 1996, President Bill Clinton endorsed dress codes in schools in his State of the Union address. A trend toward dress codes was already in progress, and some public schools were adopting uniforms. In Long Beach, California, the school district set down uniform requirements in all elementary and middle schools. School uniforms caught on in California as a way to hinder gang activity and violence. Some school districts set down a district-wide uniform, while others set down standardized dress codes, which limit certain articles of dress and styles thought to be disruptive or distracting.

In the positive view, uniforms and dress codes make kids feel less isolated. They end the competition among students to wear latest designer fashions and sport the most fashionable labels. This helps students focus on their studies as well. School uniforms limit expenses, as students don't buy as many different articles of clothing. This helps take the financial pressure off families as well. Supporters also believe uniforms help reinforce school spirit and a sense of community. Moreover, the use of uniforms in schools would help to conceal gang membership.

School officials also believe dress codes can prevent violence. Like most high schools, Columbine High School was permissive about clothing. Students could wear just about whatever they wanted, including long coats. In 1999, two students went on a shooting rampage at the school, killing twelve people before committing suicide. The two killers at Columbine had concealed their weapons underneath long trench coats.

Middle Eastern Style

They have a pretty strict dress code, at least for women, in the Middle Eastern nation of Saudi Arabia. There, women going out in public have to wear the abaya, a long black robe that completely covers (and hides) the body. Even U.S. military servicewomen were supposed to wear it, at least before 2002. That was the year the army dropped its requirement that women follow the code while out and about (women were still prohibited from driving cars or going out with men they weren't married to). The decision caused a scandal. The Saudi government promised to keep patrolling the streets for women wearing Western clothes. Groups of religious patrolmen, known as the mutawayeen, gave stern lectures and even arrested women who weren't following the code.

Supporters of uniforms believe they improve students' morale and performance. They point out that a uniform ends the daily morning agony over choosing what clothes to wear, which also helps students show up on time. They also believe that uniforms give schools a more businesslike atmosphere and help students to concentrate on their studies and take classes more seriously. Opponents of uniforms believe they are an ineffective and cosmetic method of dealing with behavioral and disciplinary issues in the schools.

Most teachers, principals, and parents support dress codes. People against dress codes believe that schools with dress codes have just as many problems as those without. They believe teachers have better things to do than watch out for what students are wearing and then bust them if they see a violation. Opponents also see dress as a form of personal expression, which everyone has a right to (at least in the United States). Some states, such as

Getting the Hang of Fashion and Dress Codes

Massachusetts, have banned dress codes in public schools, although this state allows schools to ban clothing that "violates reasonable standards of health, safety, and cleanliness."[2]

A student debater put it like this:

> Why SHOULD schools uniformly enforce their
> dress code? I'm personally against dress codes.
> They might be better than school uniforms, but
> still, if there's no law against it, I feel students
> should have the right to wear what they want. And
> look how they want. Heck, if a boy wants to come
> into school in a dress, all the power to him.[3]

Tinkering With the First Amendment

Schools in all states have to be careful about banning certain kinds of clothes or other articles such as T-shirts and arm-bands. The U.S. Constitution guarantees free speech, even to high-school students. Clothes, in some cases, mean speech, at least according to the U.S. Supreme Court. It all goes back to the famous case of *Tinker* v. *Des Moines School District*.

It was December 1965, and the United States was fighting in Vietnam, a country in Southeast Asia divided between a Communist north and U.S.-allied south. John Tinker and Christopher Eckhardt were going to high school, while John's little sister, Mary Beth, was in junior high. Like many people,

While most public schools in the United States do not require uniforms, many have fairly strict dress codes in an attempt to promote equality and improve student behavior.

Getting the Hang of Fashion and Dress Codes

the members of the Tinker and Eckhardt families were opposed to the war. After holding a meeting at the Eckhardt home, a group of students decided to wear black armbands to school to show their opposition.

The five high-school principals in Des Moines got wind of the plan. They didn't want any political issues causing a fracas in the halls and classrooms, so they tried to head it off. They said that if any student was caught wearing an armband, he or she would have to take it off. Not cooperating would mean a suspension until the student got rid of the armband.

Mary Beth, John, Christopher, and several dozen other students wore the black armbands anyway. The principals sent them home, as promised. (Several elementary students, including the younger Tinker children, also wore them to school but were not suspended.) The students stayed home for the rest of the year, and did not come back until after New Year's Day. Then their parents filed a lawsuit in federal court. The court decided against them, ruling that school principals had a right to prevent disruption in their schools.

The parents appealed the decision. They said that peacefully wearing armbands wasn't disrupting school in any way. In 1969, the case went all the way to the Supreme Court, which decided against the school and for the students. The justices made a couple of important points in their opinion.

First, wearing armbands is a passive activity that doesn't disrupt school activities or interfere with the rights of others. That means the First Amendment protects it ("free speech" can mean many things besides speech; it can be any expression of opinion, in any form). Second, the fact that the students

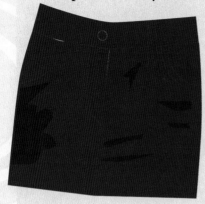

were not yet adults did not mean they didn't have their First Amendment rights, just like any other citizen who happened to be older than eighteen.

While *Tinker* v. *Des Moines* resolved the question of arm bands, the debate over dress codes rages on. School districts have the right to enforce them, in most states, and no Supreme Court decision has found them to be unconstitutional.

Fashion and style remain a very personal thing, especially in the younger years. Watch out when you try to control it, or predict it, or make a profit from it. The trend will happen and the fashion will change, outside of anyone's control. That's what makes it fun.

Getting the Hang of Fashion and Dress Codes

Chapter Notes

Chapter 1: Why Fashion?

1. Ludovica Segrebondi, "Clothes and Teenagers: What Young Men Wore in Fifteenth-Century Florence," in *The Premodern Teenager: Youth in Society, 1150—1650*, ed. Konrad Eisenbichler (Toronto, Ontario: Victoria University Centre for Reformation and Renaissance Studies, 2002), p. 29.

2. "Fashion Quotes," *The Quotations Page,* n.d., <http://www.quotationspage.com/subjects/fashion/> (May 17, 2011).

Chapter 2: Generations at the Gap

1. "28 Zoot Suiters Seized on Coast after Clashes With Service Men," *New York Times,* June 7, 1943, <http://web.viu.ca/davies/H324War/Zootsuit.riots.media.1943.htm> (May 17, 2011).

2. Skip Stone, "The Way of the Hippy," *Hippy.com,* December 1, 2001, <http://www.hippy.com/hippyway.htm> (May 17, 2011).

3. Malcolm McLaren, "Punk Rock: 30 Years of Subversion," *BBC News,* August 18, 2006, <http://news.bbc.co.uk/2/hi/entertainment/5263364.stm> (May 17, 2011).

4. "Hot Topic Inc.," *CustomerServiceNumbers.com*, n.d., <http://customerservicenumbers.com/co-hot-topic-inc-> (May 19, 2011).

Chapter 3. U.S. Dress

1. Debbi Voller, *Madonna: The Style Book* (London: Omnibus Press, 1999), p. 17.

2. R. Carmen, "Madonna Experience: A. U.S. Icon Awakens a Puerto Rican Adolescent's Feminist Consciousness," *Frontiers,* 2001, <http://find articles.com/p/articles/mi_qa3687/is_/ai_n8945323> (November 5, 2008).

3. "Emo Style–What Is It?" *Putuka.com,* n.d., <http://www.putuka.com/fashion_kulture_article.php?pag_actual=3&lang=EN&id=2> (November 7, 2008).

4. Andy Radin, "Fashion Tips," *Fourfa.com,* n.d., <http://www.fourfa.com/fashion.htm> (November 11, 2008).

Chapter 4. What's Your Style?

1. "Teen Fashion Flair Is a Family Affair—Shopzilla Survey Reveals That Teenagers Find Shopping Partners in Celebrities and Parents When It Comes to Prom Time," *Business Wire,* March 20, 2006, <http://findarticles.com/p/articles/mi_m0EIN/is_2006_March_20/ai_n16109590> (November 1, 2008).

Chapter 5. Boys, Girls, Teenagers, and Marketing

1. Anthony Burgess, *You've Had Your Time* (London: William Heinemann Ltd., 1990).

2. George Abrahams and Sheila Ahlbrand, *Boy v. Girl?* (Minneapolis, Minn.: Free Spirit Publishing, 2002), p. 10.

3. "The Merchants of Cool" transcript, *PBS*, February 27, 2001, <http://www.pbs.org/wgbh/pages/frontline/shows/cool/etc/script.html> (November 5, 2008).

4. Laura J. Buddenberg and Kathleen M. McGee, *Who's Raising Your Child?* (Boys Town, Nebr.: Boys Town Press, 2004), p. 63.

5. Abrahams and Ahlbrand, p. 110.

6. Stephen Bayley, *Taste: The Meaning of Things* (New York: Pantheon Books, 1992), p. 157.

7. Malcolm Gladwell, "The Coolhunt," *New Yorker*, March 17, 1997, <http://www.gladwell.com/1997/1997_03_17_a_cool.htm> (May 17, 2011).

8. Walter Schneider, "*The Coolhunt* and *The Merchants of Cool*," *Fathers For Life*, December 3, 2002, <http://fathersforlife.org/culture/coolhunt.htm> (November 2, 2008).

Chapter 6. Rag Trades

1. Doris Hajewski, "Kohl's Pulls Clothing; Factory Abuse Alleged," *Journal Sentinel,* June 29, 2007, <http://www.jsonline.com/business/29473734.html> (May 17, 2011).

2. Tim Dewane, "Kohl's, Sweatshop Abuse, and Daisy Fuentes Clothing," *Catholics for Peace and Justice,* n.d., <http://catholicsforpeaceandjustice.org/doc/kohlsfuentessweatshop.pdf> (November 4, 2008).

3. Ibid.

Chapter 7. The Dreaded Dress Code

1. "Enforcing Statutes of Apparel," *Elizabethan Era,* n.d., <http://www.elizabethan-era.org.uk/enforcing-statutes-of-apparel.htm> (October 15, 2008).

2. "Dress Codes and School-Uniform Policies, State by State," *University of Oregon,* n.d., <http://eric.uoregon.edu/publications/policy_reports/dress_codes/statebystate.html> (May 17, 2011).

3. "Hardly Fair: A Silly School Dress Code Debate," *Debate.org,* n.d., <http://www.debate.com/debates/Hardly-Fair-A-Silly-School-Dress-Code-Debate/1/> (November 10, 2008).

Glossary

abaya—A long black robe that completely covers the body, worn in Saudi Arabia.

barrio—A Spanish-speaking neighborhood in a U.S. city.

grembiule—A smock-like garment worn by Italian schoolgirls.

haute couture (literally, "high fashion")—Clothing based on original designs and made in only a few samples.

hijab—A headscarf worn by Muslim women.

mass market—Inexpensive clothing; less expensive and less well made than ready-to-wear.

pachuco—A young Mexican American belonging to a neighborhood gang.

ready-to-wear—Clothing made from original designs in large lots, in specific sizes, and sold through retail stores.

sumptuary laws—Laws limiting extravagant expenditures on luxury items.

sweatshop—A factory in which people work in poor conditions for little pay.

zoot suit—A suit popular in the 1940s consisting of a long jacket with wide shoulders and pants with narrow cuffs.

Further Reading

Craats, Rennay. *Fashion: USA—Past, Present, Future*. New York: Weigl Publishers, 2009.

Jones, Jen. *Fashion History: Looking Great Through the Ages*. Mankato, Minn.: Capstone Press, 2007.

Jones, Jen. *Fashion Trends: How Popular Style Is Shaped*. Mankato, Minn.: Capstone Press, 2007.

Stalder, Erika. *Fashion 101: A Crash Course in Clothing*. San Francisco, Calif.: Zest Books, 2008.

Wallach, Marlene, with Grace Norwich. *My Look: A Guide to Fashion & Style*. New York: Aladdin Mix, 2009.

Getting the Hang of Fashion and Dress Codes

Clothing: Academic Kids Encyclopedia
<http://academickids.com/encyclopedia/index.
php/Clothing>

The History of Clothing
<http://inventors.about.com/od/
cstartinventions/a/clothing.htm>

Love to Know: Teen Fashion
<http://teens.lovetoknow.com/Category:Teen_
Fashion>

Index

Getting the Hang of Fashion and Dress Codes